Contending
for your
Faith
in these
Times

Katrina Johnson

Contending for your *Faith* in these Times

Copyright © 2022 by Katrina Johnson

Social Media:
Email: 2contend4faith@gmail.com
Instagram: contending4yourfaith
Facebook: Contend 4 Your Faith
Twitter: Contend4Faith1

All rights reserved. No part of this book may be reproduced or transmitted in any form, written or electronic or by any means, electronic or mechanical, including photocopying, recording, or by any information storage and retrieval system, without written consent from the author.

ISBN: 978-0-9850914-8-4

Printed in the United States of America

Cover designed by:

Spectrum Paradigm
Consulting & Services, Inc.

Versions of the Bible taken from the International Bible Society (IBS) and are indicated by 3 letter abbreviations including Amplified Bible, Amplified Bible Classic edition (AMPC), New International Version (NIV), King James Version (KJV) or Easy-to-Read version. IBS-STL Global ©2008. All Rights Reserved Worldwide.

Excellence Publishing

Contents

Introduction ---5

Chapter 1: Staying Grounded in Our Common Salvation --------------------7

Chapter 2: What Does it Mean to Contend for Your Faith ------------------15

Chapter 3: Get Suited! ---19

Chapter 4: Contending to Fulfill Your Purpose ----------------------------------31

Chapter 5: Work out Your Own Salvation with Reverential Fear -------39

Chapter 6: Contending for Your Faith after Tragedy ---------------------------49

Chapter 7: How Will You Contend for Your Faith? ------------------------------55

References ---59

Introduction

Accepting Jesus Christ as Lord and Savior is the best decision we can make for our lives. In doing so, we initiate a new life in God. We make a conscious decision to dedicate our lives to the Word of God. The Word of God is our blueprint for Holy and victorious living. In addition to God's written word, we have a Comforter, who is the Holy Spirit, who leads and guides us into all truth.

As we have the Word of God and His help to live as God intended, we have a responsibility to work out our own salvation and finish the course that has been set before us. We are to take up our cross daily by crucifying the flesh and dying to sinful mindsets. As believers, we have a responsibility to speak and defend God's Word, which is the ultimate truth.

This book will teach you how to contend for your faith and live in victory. After reading this book, you will be inspired to stand firm in your faith, defend truth, and share the love and salvation of God through Jesus Christ.

CHAPTER 1

STAYING GROUNDED IN OUR COMMON SALVATION

Acts 4:12 ERV
*Jesus is the only one who can save people.
His name is the only power in the world
that has been given to save anyone.
We must be saved through Him!"*

What is Common Salvation & What We Believe

Before we address "Contending for our Faith", I want us to review our "Common Salvation." We understand God gave His only begotten Son, Jesus Christ, to die on the Cross for our sins. Jesus Christ shed His blood, and He was crucified. Jesus was buried and resurrected. Through Jesus' death and resurrection, we have remission of our sins. Salvation belongs to those who confess with their mouths and believe that Jesus Christ is Lord!

There is no other name in which men or women can be saved. These facts are non-negotiable. This is the foundation of our faith. However, there are voices throughout the earth attempting to deceive humanity into thinking there is more than one way to access God. Therefore, it is imperative that we remember what our "Common Salvation" is and continue in the doctrine of truth. We must be aware of deception through heresies.

Beware of Heresies

The book of Jude was written to warn believers about evil individuals, who infiltrated the church with false doctrine and heresies. Jude identified them as, *"ungodly men, who turn the grace of our God into lewdness and deny the only Lord*

God and our Lord Jesus Christ." Let's look at the root word of heresies. The root word of heresies is **heresy.** Heresy is defined *as dissent or deviation from a dominant theory, opinion, or practice*. It also means *an opinion, doctrine, or practice contrary to the truth*. An example of a heresy is a belief shared from a prestigious religious leader on several occasions. He expressed his belief that all of the major religions are different paths to the same God. Renowned teachers, preachers and celebrities are also misleading individuals that different religions provide salvation and eternal life. There's only one path to God, which provides salvation and everlasting life according to John 14:6 ESV, which states, "Jesus answered, *"I am the way, the truth, and the life. The only way to the Father is through me."*

A Strange Voice or False Doctrine You Will Not Follow

I define a **strange voice**, as *a sound or communication that is antagonistic to Christ or not conducive to the Word of God*. The source of the strange voice is the devil. This strange voice leads you away from foundational truths or facts. A strange voice will normally lead individuals to idolatry, mayhem, confusion, or opposition to Holiness. Strange voices lead to worshiping false gods and doing worthless, religious acts. Strange voices can also clog our ears from adhering to the truth. An example of a worthless act would be burning sage to clean your house of evil spirits. According to Mark 16:17, we are to cast out evil spirits in the name of Jesus. Burning sage will not expel evil spirits. This practice will actually make you more susceptible to demonic attack because you are relying on a paganistic ritual instead of the power of Jesus Christ and His blood.

Do not be deceived by strange voices that attempt to lead you away from biblical truths. To avoid being deceived, get grounded in your Word. Study the Word of God and stay connected with the Heavenly Father through prayer and worship. Submit to leaders in ministry that are committed to Christ and sound doctrine as it relates to our common salvation. If your pastor or leader starts justifying sin or encourages you to commit idolatrous practices, such as, burning bowls, offering prayers to idols, consulting psychics or mediums, run fast to avoid being devoured or deceived by the enemy. You should only seek spiritual knowledge from the Holy Spirit that aligns in God's Word and ultimate truth.

The Bible talks about how the devil is seeking whom he can devour. Let's look at the Contemporary English Version of 1 Peter 5:8. It reads: *"Be on your guard and stay awake. Your enemy, the devil, is like a roaring lion, sneaking around to find someone to attack."* I believe the enemy attempts to take advantage of believers during vulnerable or difficult times in an attempt to make us deny Jesus Christ and fall back into sin. If we are not careful, we will be taken advantage of by the enemy and miss out on God's best for our lives. It's imperative that we strengthen our inner man to remain faithful to Jesus Christ.

Ephesians 3:16 AMP reads:

"16 May He grant you out of the riches of His glory, to be strengthened and spiritually energized with power through His Spirit in your inner self, [indwelling your innermost being and personality], 17 so that Christ may dwell in your hearts through your faith. And may you, having been [deeply] rooted and [securely] grounded in love, 18 be fully capable of comprehending with all the saints (God's people) the width and length and height and depth of His love [fully experiencing that amazing, endless love]; 19 and [that you may come] to know [practically, through personal experience] the love of Christ which far surpasses [mere] knowledge [without experience], that you may be filled up [throughout your being] to all the fullness of God [so that you

may have the richest experience of God's presence in your lives, completely filled and flooded with God Himself]."

The Rise of Polytheism

Polytheism is becoming more prevalent in these times. The word **polytheism** means *the belief in or worship of more than one god.* Polytheism comes from the Greek word poly+theoi, literally is "many gods." Most ancient religions were polytheistic or worshipped more than one God for various reasons, such as to attain prosperity, achieve peace, make sacrificial offerings, or keep traditions. Polytheism is happening today. Unknowingly, there are believers in the Body of Christ that practice religious customs contrary to our Christian faith today. Any rituals, religious practices or chants that denounce Christ as Lord or replace Christ and the Power of the Holy Ghost is idolatry. Let's read what the Apostle Paul wrote to the early church regarding idolatry.

The Apostle Paul wrote in 1 Corinthians 8:5-6 New International Version (NIV): *"For even if there are so-called gods, whether in heaven or on earth (as indeed there are many "gods" and many "lords"), 6 yet for us there is but one God, the Father, from whom all things came and for whom we live; and there is but one Lord, Jesus Christ, through whom all things came and through whom we live."*

The Apostle Paul reinforced for us as believers. There is only one God, the Father and we serve Him through Jesus Christ.

The Great Falling Away

Recent studies conducted by the Pew Research Center identified that a growing share of Americans are religiously unaffiliated. There was a sample share of 1,300 individuals used for this study. Simply put, a lot of individuals are choosing not to identify with a religion or church because of skepticism. I believe there is a lot of skepticism due to the hypocrisy of religious affiliates, churches, or lack of life changing power.

However, I believe God is raising up a remnant of believers who will teach and preach the gospel of Jesus Christ with the anointed power of the Holy Ghost to demonstrate tangible healings, deliverance, and miracles to prove Jesus Christ is Lord. My prayer is that in these days, we will walk in the demonstrative power of God! As we demonstrate the Kingdom of God in power, many will believe that we serve a true and living God through Jesus Christ, our Savior. That's why we must stay grounded in our common salvation. Please complete the follow up exercise on the next page.

Follow-Up Exercise

Describe in your own words, what is our *Common Salvation*?

_____

_____

_____

_____

What will you do to make sure you will not be deceived by false doctrine?

_____

_____

_____

_____

Write down your final thoughts or key take-aways regarding Chapter 1:

_____

_____

_____
_____
_____

CHAPTER 2

WHAT DOES IT MEAN TO CONTEND FOR YOUR FAITH

What Does It Mean to Contend for Your Faith?

To contend means *to fight or execute action for something or someone.* Additional definitions for **contend** from Merriam-Webster dictionary defines **contend** as, *"to strive or vie in contest or rivalry or against difficulties. To strive or debate. "To maintain, assert. To struggle for or to contest."* I like how CollinsDictionary.com defines **contend**. It reads, *"If you have to contend with a problem or difficulty, you have to deal with it or overcome it. If you contend that something is true, you state or argue that it is true. If you contend with someone for something such as power, you compete with them to try and get it."*

Why Do We Contend for Our Faith?

We contend for our faith to continue with Christ and walk in all the promises God has for us. We contend for our faith, so we do not shift away from the gospel. We contend to inherit His blessings. We contend so we can be an example to win others over to the Gospel. We contend so we will receive a crown of Glory. We contend that God's will, which is in Heaven, is done in the earth. We contend to demonstrate the power of His Kingdom and His righteousness now. The list goes on and on. The bottom line, we contend for our faith to receive our expected end, which is victory and eternal life with Christ as indicated in Revelation 2:7 (KJV), which reads, *"He that hath an ear, let him hear what the Spirit saith unto the churches; To him that overcome will I give to eat of the tree of life, which is in the midst of the paradise of God."*

Who are our enemies?

To successfully contend for your faith, you need to know who your real spiritual enemy is. As humans, we tend to believe our enemies are in the flesh. However, Ephesians 6:12 states, *"we are not fighting flesh and blood but principalities and spiritual wickedness in high places."* Our enemies are fallen angels sent on assignment to steal, kill, or destroy our destiny or purpose. These spiritual enemies use people to attack our faith, our hearts, our physical bodies, and our mental health. The devil's job is to frustrate us, make us deny the truth and walk away from God. Sure, we suffer attacks from mankind on every side. There are some really evil people carrying out despicable acts. Or it seems their main purpose is to cause distress to the people of God. But no worries. If we are in Christ, we have the ultimate victory, if we keep our guards up!

The Bible talks about how the devil is seeking whom he can devour. Let's look at the Contemporary English Version of I Peter 5:8. It reads, *"Be on your guard and stay awake. Your enemy, the devil, is like a roaring lion, sneaking around to find someone to attack."* I believe the enemy attempts to take advantage of believers during vulnerable or difficult times, in an attempt to make us deny Jesus Christ and fall back into sin. If we are not careful, we will be taken advantage of by the enemy and miss out on God's best for our lives.

We are to stay alert. How do we stay alert? Be engaged with the Lord on a daily basis. Watch and pray without ceasing. Stay connected with your local assembly and fellowship with the saints. Be a student of the Word of God. Above all things, hear the Word of God and keep it. Before you start your day, pray, and put on the Full Armor of God, piece by piece. You will do this by speaking it out of your mouth. The next chapter will provide further details about putting on the

Full Armor of God according to God's Word. For now, please complete the follow-up exercise on the next page.

Follow-Up Exercise

Describe in your own words, what does it mean to *Contend for your Faith*?

_____

_____

_____

_____

Why is it important to *Contend for Your Faith*?

_____

_____

_____

_____

Write down your final thoughts or key-take-aways regarding Chapter 2:

_____

_____

CHAPTER 3

GET SUITED!

The Importance to Prepare for Battle to Contend for Your Faith

The Apostle Paul wrote to believers in Ephesus about preparing for battle or spiritual warfare to overcome trials, temptation, and persecution. The Apostle Paul encouraged believers in Ephesus to "put on the whole armor of God" so believers could stand firm in their faith. I encourage you to literally pray Ephesians 6:13-18. The Full Armor of God is a spiritual uniform to prepare you for battle. Let's take a brief look at the Full Armor of God. It is listed in order according to scripture. At the end of this chapter, there is a prayer to put on the Full Armor of God, daily.

Belt of Truth

The first piece of armor mentioned in Ephesians 6:14, is the belt of truth. We are told to gird our loins with truth. Loins are considered a seat of strength. According to vocabulary.com, **gird** is defined as, *"to prepare for a military attack, but more loosely it refers to readying yourself for any kind of confrontation. When you gird for something, you are preparing for the worst-case scenario."* As believers, we are to strengthen our core with God's Word, so we can be ready to handle or endure anything life throws at us. This means being prepared for confrontation from the enemy, whether it is physical, mental, or spiritual.

Remember, the Word says Satan is the father of lies and there is no truth in him. So, the enemy is going to come with lies, such as, God doesn't love you or He is not going to keep His promises to you. You need to understand, beyond a shadow of a doubt, that God is faithful and true to His Word. The enemy will also attempt to deceive us with false doctrine. We must know **who** we believe in and **why**, so we will not be led astray. Having your core or loins girded with the Belt of Truth will give you endurance to remain stable in God's Word.

The Breastplate of Righteousness

The second piece of armor we are to put on is the Breastplate of Righteousness. The Breastplate of Righteousness protects our hearts. Proverbs 4:23 (NKJV) reads, *"Keep your heart with all diligence, for out of it spring the issues of life."* You must have a heart that is pure. You must make sure you are not holding unforgiveness, bitterness or resentment in your heart. If your heart is not guarded or protected when tests, trials or persecution comes, your heart can become hardened and negative responses can flow from your heart, such as anger, murmuring and complaining. If your heart is not protected with all diligence, it can fail you. If we do not protect our hearts, it is possible we will stray from walking in the Spirit and concede to the lust of the flesh. If we do not put on the Breastplate of Righteousness, we can incur wounds that hinder our spiritual growth.

Feet in Preparation with the Gospel of Peace

We are to walk with the purpose of sharing the Gospel of Jesus Christ and the ministry of reconciliation. Before we can share the Gospel with others, we must prepare ourselves in prayer and knowledge of God's Word. The Bible says, God's Word is a lamp unto our feet and a light unto our path. The Gospel we represent, we preach, and we teach comes with assurance. It comes with a message to bring humanity into the peace of God by Jesus Christ.

The Shield of Faith

The Shield of Faith is one of the most important weapons we can use daily. During our lives, we will have attacks from the enemy. These attacks can come from the very pit of hell to detour you. To quench the fiery darts of the enemy attacks, you must use faith. **Quench** means *to extinguish; to put out; as, to quench flame*. Dictionary.com defines **quench** as, *to subdue, destroy or overcome*. We need to remember the attacks may seem to be intense or fiery, but we have already overcome through Jesus Christ. We just need to quench the lies, deceit, and attacks through faith.

Faith is belief or hope in what God's Word has said about you, your outcome, and His promises. Faith says that God is good, and He is faithful regardless of what is going on in our lives. Faith says, *"All things work together for good to those who love God."* Lastly, faith says, we are more than conquerors.

The Helmet of Salvation & Your Mindset

The mind is where most strongholds are. The mind is where doubt, anxiety and unbelief can overwhelm believers. We must take the Helmet of Salvation to guard our mind. The Helmet of Salvation is a protective shield in the Spirit. Putting on the Helmet of Salvation helps us make a conscious effort to guard our thoughts and keep Christ at the forefront of our thoughts. It is having the "Mind of Christ." The Mind of Christ refers to the thoughts, reverence or admonishment of God's Word and power. The Helmet of Salvation protects your mind from condemnation and lies of the devil. With the Helmet of Salvation, you will be protected from the "blows to the head" from the enemy. Most battles happen in the mind. If you meditate on God's Word and protect your mind, you will have your mind right and make it to the finish line.

The Wrong Mindset is a Threat!

As a believer, you must know that God has good thoughts towards you. He loves you. He has plans for you. Thoughts of good and not of evil and to bring you to an expected end. Many believers have moved away from the Lord or feel that God has let them down because they truly do not have a revelation of God's love and will for their lives. Regardless of what happens in our lives, we must be resolute in knowing that God is Holy and good. He wants the best for us, and He never leaves or forsakes us. When you go through your next trials, make sure you think about how God spared His only begotten Son to live and die on the cross for our sins. Jesus suffered insurmountable persecution and rejection. The Bible says, He was a man of many sorrows. God the Father allowed Jesus, Son of God to suffer and die for our sins for the greater good, which was, salvation for humanity. We suffer for righteousness's sake and for God's glory to be revealed.

What's Your State of Mind?

Now more than ever, believers in the Body of Christ are suffering from anxiety. I am not referring to chemical imbalances diagnosed from a psychologist. There are believers actually experiencing anxiety from a place of fear. Fear of the unknown. Fear of failure. Fear of rejection. Fear of death. Fear of condemnation. Some believers cannot receive the love of God because of their distorted thinking about God or themselves.

I have prayed for many individuals plagued with this form of anxiety because they did not truly understand God's unconditional love, and His good thoughts towards them. My favorite scripture to declare and minister deliverance is 2 Timothy which states, *"For God hath not given us the spirit of fear; but of power, and of love, and of a sound mind."* It is important to meditate on God's Word to have a sound mind to counter attack the lies from the devil.

Think on These Things!

The Word of God says in Philippians 4:8 ESV:

"Finally, brothers, whatever is true, whatever is honorable, whatever is just, whatever is pure, whatever is lovely, whatever is commendable, if there is any excellence, if there is anything worthy of praise, think about these things."

Have the right mindset daily. This includes having thoughts regarding the will of God, holiness, and walking in excellence. Having Godly thoughts will bring excellence to your life. It will cause you to live righteously. And, from righteous living comes the momentum to walk in the ordained power and anointing that God has given you, so the enemy cannot defeat you in your mind.

Sword of the Spirit - The Word of God

The Sword of the Spirit is powerful. It is God's Word. It is a weapon that can be used in offense <u>or</u> defense. In the "offense" usage of the word ***weapon***, get in the habit of quoting or decreeing scriptures throughout the day to build your faith. If you are believing God to save your family, decree this from Acts 2:39 which reads, *"For the promise is unto you, and to your children, and to all that are afar off, even as many as the Lord our God shall call."* Just quote the Word of God. Quote the Word of God until you see the manifestation of your loved ones being saved or you walking in God's purpose for your life.

In the "defense" usage of the word ***weapon***, when the enemy comes, we need to state what the Word of God says about our situation. Next, we need to do what the Word says to do. Listen, I've been there. That's why I'm writing about it; to help others. The Word of God works! We need to study God's Word to learn God's character and His will for your life. We need God's Word saturated in our lives, so we can use it when attacks come. Jesus gave a perfect example of how He used the Sword of the Spirit when He was tempted by the enemy. Jesus quoted the Word and Satan had to flee. Strike the enemy with the sword of the Lord, which is the Word of the Lord.

Jesus Example of Using the Sword of the Spirit in the Wilderness

The Bible states Jesus was led by the Spirit into the wilderness to be tempted by the devil. The devil tempted Him on three occasions. First, the devil came to tempt Jesus with food. Of course, Jesus was hungry after fasting forty days and forty nights. The Bible says in Matthew 4 NASB, *"The tempter came to Him and said, "If you are the Son of God, tell these stones to become bread."* Jesus used the Sword of the Spirit, which was the Word of God and said, *"It is written: 'Man shall not live on bread alone, but on every word that comes from the mouth of God."*

Second, the devil took Him to the holy city and had Him stand on the highest point of the temple. *"If you are the Son of God,"* he said, *"throw yourself down. For it is written, 'He will command His angels concerning you, and they will lift you up in their hands, so that you will not strike your foot against a stone."* Jesus used the Sword of the Spirit, which is the Word of God and said, *"It is also written: 'Do not put the Lord your God to the test.'"*

Third, the devil took Jesus to a very high mountain and showed Him all the kingdoms of the world and their splendor. The devil said, *"All this I will give you,"* he said, *"if you will bow down and worship me."* Again, Jesus used the

Sword of the Spirit, which is the Word of God, and said to him, *"Away from me, Satan. For it is written: 'Worship the Lord your God and serve Him only."* The Word of God is our greatest weapon of power. No enemy or circumstance can overthrow God's Word.

Contend for Your Faith through Prayer, Praise and Worship

As a child of God, it is important that you stay connected to God. In order to stay connected, you need to have a strong prayer life. Commune with God through prayer. Go beyond asking God for something to possess or gain but talk to Him. Share your thoughts, desires, and feelings. Admire His majesty. Declare who God is. Worship Him with a song. Abide with Him as a friend. Intimacy with God is key. To fight, stand strong to endure to the end. You must maintain your relationship with God.

Prayer and Fasting is Essential

Prayer is communication with God. Fasting is abstinence from food or drink for a dedicated or extended period of time. Prayer involves worship, repentance, petition and surrender to God's will. Fasting causes you to get control of your flesh or put your flesh (human nature/physical body) under constraint. Prayer and fasting should be constant. Prayer and fasting are important to contend for your faith. Without a prayer life, it will be difficult to win battles. Stay connected with God and grow in grace.

During Jesus' life on earth, He always prayed. Jesus was always able to keep focus on His assignment. The disciples observed how Jesus had perseverance, power, and authority. The disciples observed how Jesus prayed so much, one of the disciples asked Jesus to teach them how to pray, according to Luke 11:1 which says, *"And it came to pass, that, as He was praying in a certain place, when He ceased, one of His disciples said unto him, 'Lord, teach us to pray, as John also taught His disciples.'"* Prayer and fasting will help you endure during times of trials, tribulations, and persecution.

Taking it Up a Notch-Spiritual Warfare

The Bible states that we have a spiritual enemy we need to contend with. That enemy is the devil. The enemy is seeking to control and hijack believers from reaching their potential. Ephesians 6:12 (AMP) reads, *"For our struggle is not against flesh and blood [contending only with physical opponents], but against the rulers, against the powers, against the world forces of this [present] darkness, against the spiritual forces of wickedness in the heavenly (supernatural) places."* How do we contend with the enemy? Through spiritual warfare and prayer.

It's important that we are not ignorant of Satan's devices. Every day, we need to bind up the enemy and decree victory in Jesus Christ. We need to rebuke the enemy when he comes with foolishness. Exercise your authority according to Luke 10:19 AMP which states, *"Listen carefully: I have given you authority [that you now possess] to tread on [a]serpents and scorpions, and [the ability to exercise authority] over all the power of the enemy (Satan); and nothing will [in any way] harm you."*

Contend for Your Families, Friends, and Loved Ones

There's a spiritual enemy that's in the world seeking whom he can devour. It's the devil. He is on his job 24 hours a day to steal, kill and destroy. To contend for the faith, we must pray against the works of the enemy. We must cover our families, friends, co-workers, neighbors, and others in prayer. Find specific scriptures in the Word to pray over your family, friends, neighborhood, or region.

One of my favorite scriptures to pray over my family is Isaiah 54:17 NIV, *"No weapon forged against you will prevail, and you will refute every tongue that accuses you." This is the heritage of the servants of the LORD, and this is their vindication from me," declares the LORD.* Replace the word "you" with your name or your family's name.

Prayer to Put on the Full Armor of God

In the name of Jesus, we put on the Belt of Truth, which causes the core of our being to be secured in the Word of God. We decree the Belt of Truth will keep us grounded no matter what happens today. We will not be uprooted because the Belt of Truth secures us. Our core, our inner man is rooted and grounded by what the Word of God says I am. I am stable today because I have a strong core in Jesus Christ.

In the name of Jesus, we put on the Breastplate of Righteousness. Our Breastplate of Righteousness will protect our heart from lustful desires. Our heart is protected against thoughts, feelings, or emotions contrary to the Holy Word of God. Our Breastplate of Righteousness will protect us from being bitter from rejection, persecution, hardships, or disappointments.

In the name of Jesus, we put the Gospel of Peace on our feet. We will bring hope and reconciliation to others through the Word of God. Wherever we go, we will bring hope, love, and God's peace to those in need. We will share the Gospel of Jesus Christ and demonstrate the power of God's Kingdom. God's Word will be a light unto our path, and it will give us opportunities to share the Gospel of Jesus Christ.

In the name of Jesus, we put on the Shield of Faith. The Shield of Faith will quench every dart and lie of the enemy. Satan's attacks will not pierce through our armor. We will not be spiritually devastated or wounded. We will not be overtaken by the enemy. Regardless of any fiery darts coming our way, through faith, weapons from the enemy cannot penetrate our armor. Fiery darts will boomerang off us. Our Shield of Faith, through God's Word will keep us secure while we stand firm believing God is faithful.

In the name of Jesus, we put on the Helmet of Salvation. The Helmet of Salvation will guard our minds from every mental attack and lie from the devil. I will have the mind of Christ because my mind is guarded with the knowledge of salvation and truth.

In the name of Jesus, we take our Sword of the Spirit, which is the Word of God. We strike our sword against every foe, against every attack, every lie and stronghold, in Jesus name.

Let's gauge your level of understanding related to "Getting Suited" to contend for your faith on a daily basis on the next page.

Follow-Up Exercise

What does it mean to "Get Suited" with the *Full Armor of God*?

_____
_____
_____
_____
_____

What piece of the *Full Armor of God* do you feel is most important to put on daily? Why?

_____
_____
_____
_____
_____

Why is it important to prepare for battle daily?

_____
_____

Write down your final thoughts or key take-aways regarding Chapter 3:

CHAPTER 4

CONTENDING TO FULFILL YOUR PURPOSE

As a believer, we have God's Holy Spirit abiding in us. His anointing shines on our countenance. We are a force to be reckoned with. Because of Christ, we make the devil tremble or feel quite uncomfortable in the spirit realm. Because of our anointing and God's grace upon us, we irritate devils. I hope this paragraph conveys the point I am making as it relates to the power that resides in us!

The Word says in 1 Peter 4:14 AMP, *"If you are insulted and reviled for [bearing] the name of Christ, you are blessed [happy, with life-joy and comfort in God's salvation regardless of your circumstances], because the Spirit of glory and of God is resting on you [and indwelling you—He whom they curse, you glorify]."*

As believers, we will suffer for righteousness' sake as we attempt to live for Christ. Mistreatment may occur through various channels, such as the marketplace, school, or organization. Consider the last two paragraphs. Hopefully, this provides some reasoning for any attacks, hostility, envy, jealousy, persecution, slander, or disdain you may have experienced in the past or are experiencing now. Attacks have, can or will occur towards us simply because of who we are. I want to compel you to read this chapter as it relates to your experiences and walk in a new level of freedom and victory because of the anointing that rests upon you.

If you have not intentionally offended, injured, harmed, or committed any egregious acts against anyone, realize your trials are simply a result of you being a child of God and Satan is working overtime to frustrate, delay, disrupt or discourage you from living for Christ. It is imperative that you decree Isaiah 54:17 every day, which says: *"no weapon formed against you shall prosper. Every tongue that rises up against you shall be proven wrong."* Also meditate on Romans 12:14 which says, *"Bless them which persecute you. Bless and curse not. Executing God's Word through prayers, decrees and obedience is vital in contending for your faith."*

The Spirit of Herod

I would like to share the revelation God shared with me about the evil spirit of Herod. The spirit of Herod is sent on assignment to oppress, destroy, threaten, or hinder God's purpose, mission, or assignment on a believer's life. Many in the Body of Christ are not familiar with the spirit of Herod or have limited knowledge of this spirit because they only consider one account of Herod, which was Herod the Great, who was on assignment to kill Jesus as a baby in Matthew 2:13-15. However, there's a lineage of "King Herods" that had rule in Judea. These "Herods" always misused their position of authority to persecute, assassinate or injure believers in New Testament biblical accounts. I believe the spirit of Herod seeks to destroy ministries and individuals at different levels of maturity in an attempt to stop God's purpose or momentum in the life of believers.

What does Herod mean in Greek?

The name Herod derives from the Greek name **Herodes**, which means *"song of the hero or warrior"*. This was the name of several rulers of Judea during the period when it was part of the Roman Empire. Based on this derivative, it's a warrior spirit that fights and persecutes believers to different degrees. In my experience, this spirit fights dirty to annihilate or crush the spirit of their victims. This spirit can be at work through anyone that has governmental authority in a region, organization, or marketplace. In this book, I will share a few accounts of how this spirit attempted to obliterate God's anointed from fulfilling God's plan.

Herod the Great Attempted to Kill Jesus

Earlier in this chapter, I mentioned how Herod the Great attempted to kill Jesus as a baby, according to Matthew 2:13-15. Why did Herod want to kill an innocent baby? To abort or prevent God's covenant promises from being fulfilled. For example, the prophets of the Old Testament prophesied how Jesus would be a descendant of Abraham and through Him, generations would be blessed. The KJV of Genesis 12:3 reads, *"I will bless those who bless you, and I will curse him who curses you; and in you all the families of the earth shall be blessed."*

If Jesus died prematurely, Jesus' ministry upon the earth would not have been fulfilled according to Isaiah 61:1-2 AMP, which states: *"The Spirit of the Lord God is upon me, because the Lord has anointed and commissioned me to bring good news to the humble and afflicted; He has sent me to bind up [the wounds of] the brokenhearted, to proclaim release [from confinement and condemnation] to the [physical and spiritual] captives and freedom to prisoners, to proclaim [a]the favorable year of the Lord,] and the day of vengeance and retribution of our God, to comfort all who mourn."* It was imperative that Jesus was protected from Herod the Great so He could fulfill His ministry assignment. Read Matthew 2nd chapter to learn more about how Jesus' earthly parents were instructed to escape to Egypt to protect Jesus as an infant.

Herod Antipas Assignment against John the Baptist

In Matthew 14:3-12, Herod Antipas killed John the Baptist at the request of his niece due to lingering animosity from being confronted of his sin with his sister-in-law. That's just like the work of the enemy, as soon as a bold, righteous person confronts sin, the enemy retaliates. However, we have the victory in Christ and shall overcome any affliction the enemy attacks with, according to Psalm 34:19.

The Spirit of Herod attempted to Intimidate Jesus as an Adult through the Pharisees

The Pharisees attempted to intimidate Jesus and stop His momentum in doing Kingdom work. The Pharisees implored Jesus to run as He was heading towards Jerusalem. Luke 13:31 TLB confirms, *"A few minutes later some Pharisees said to Him, "Get out of here if you want to live, for King Herod is after you!"* I loved what Jesus said in verse 32. Jesus replied, *"Go tell that fox that I will keep on casting out demons and doing miracles of healing today and tomorrow; and the third day I will reach my destination."* This is one of my favorite responses Jesus had towards the enemy. He called Herod Antipas out and continued in ministry.

Herod Agrippa Persecution of James, Son of Zebedee and Apostle Peter

In Acts 12:1-4, Herod Agrippa (I) decided to persecute certain leaders in the church. Herod Agrippa executed Jesus' disciple James, son of Zebedee and imprisoned Peter. However, due to the fervent and persistent prayers being made to God by the believers, the angels of the Lord came to deliver Peter out of the prison. God delivered Peter out of the hands of Herod Agrippa so he could complete his assignment for the Kingdom of God. We can be assured God will deliver us as well.

I just shared three accounts in which the spirit of Herod attempted to prevent, halt, or destroy an individual's purpose or assignment. Today, the sinister attacks of the spirit of Herod manifest differently in these times. Have you ever experienced a leader that used everything at their disposal to destroy your purpose, ruin your brand or limit the scope of your work or reach? Have you been under so much oppression you were exasperated and wanted to give up? Have you ever been scrutinized by those in authority whose sole purpose was to destroy you or break your spirit?

If so, it could be the spirit of Herod at work. If so, bind up that spirit in the Name of Jesus. Ask God to release warrior angels to be dispatched on your behalf and continue to put on your whole armor of God as indicated in Chapter 3, "Get Suited to Contend in These Times." Complete the following exercise on the next page."

Follow-Up Exercise

Identify a time when you faced opposition, persecution or tribulations because of your faith or God's call on your life?

_____

_____

_____

_____

What was or has been your response to opposition, persecution, or tribulations due to God's call on your life?

_____

_____

_____

_____

What will you do differently when you experience opposition, persecution or tribulations because of your faith, God's call, or Holy Spirit's anointing on your life?

_____

_____

CHAPTER 5

WORK OUT YOUR OWN SALVATION WITH REVERENTIAL FEAR OF THE LORD

Once we accept Jesus Christ our Lord and Savior, we have the responsibility to allow God's Word to transform our lives. What does "working out your own salvation" mean? My definition of **working out your own salvation** means *total surrender to God's authority and truth to walk in Godly character.* It means applying biblical concepts to every facet of our lives so God can receive the Glory. It means receiving deliverance and freedom from demonic strongholds and continuing in your belief that Jesus Christ is Lord. It means overcoming persecution, betrayals, and tribulations. It means growing into a mature believer and to demonstrate the power of God on the earth.

Let's look at what Apostle Paul wrote to encourage believers to work out their own salvation. Philippians 2:11-13 reads:

"11 and that every tongue will confess and openly acknowledge that Jesus Christ is Lord (sovereign God), to the glory of God the Father. 12 So then, my dear ones, just as you have always obeyed [my instructions with enthusiasm], not only in my presence, but now much more in my absence, continue to work out your salvation [that is, cultivate it, bring it to full effect, actively pursue spiritual maturity] with awe-inspired fear and trembling [using serious caution and critical self-evaluation to avoid anything that might offend God or discredit the name of Christ]. 13 For it is [not your strength, but it is] [a]God who is effectively at work in you, both to will and to work [that is, strengthening, energizing, and creating in you the longing and the ability to fulfill your purpose] for His good pleasure."

We must always rely on God's grace to work out our own salvation. It is through the power of God we overcome difficulties. The grace of God gives us the grace to crucify our flesh. To crucify our flesh means to die to fleshly desires or lust. God gives more grace to the humble. James 4:6 KJV reads. "But He giveth more grace. Wherefore He saith, God resists the proud, but giveth grace unto the humble."

Why is Your Battle So Tough?

There are times in which our battle seems really intense. What I've learned is your ministry, or purpose of your anointing is related to your specific battle. Let me explain. If your battle has been in the area of persecution at the workplace, chances are, you will be promoted, become an entrepreneur, or be used by God to minister salvation and God's love in the workplace. If your battle is with your family, chances are you will evangelize them or be a spiritual covering through prayer. If your battle is in your finances, chances are, you are destined to be wealthy to bless the Kingdom of God.

So, with this in mind, this is why you would need to pray according to the Word of God. You will need to declare and speak what the Word of God says relating to your battle or circumstance. As believers, it is important that we do not have a victim or "woe is me" mentality. We must rise up and say to ourselves, *"God has a purpose to strengthen, mature or bless us in the area of our pain points or trials."* It is important that we contend for our faith during our battles, so we can walk into the purpose God has ordained for us.

Contending for Your Faith During Difficult Times

In this current age, many are denying Jesus Christ is Lord because of heartache, disappointment, or worldly desires. Some individuals are denying the faith because of what they perceive as an unanswered prayer from God. Others feel that God does not love them because of a tragic event, such as the death of a loved one or loss of material possessions. In actuality, bad events may have occurred because of the devil or life's choices and/or consequences. In spite of what happens in our lives, God is good and wants His best for our lives. However, the devil does not. The Word tells us the enemy came to steal, kill, or destroy but Jesus said, *"I come that you might have life and life more abundantly,"* in John 10:10. If you do not know and believe in your heart that Jesus wants you to have an abundant life filled with joy, peace, health, you are at risk of being discouraged and not persevering during trials. Please understand, according to John 10:11, Jesus stated, *"I am a good shepherd and I give life to my sheep."* You must believe that He is a Good Shepherd regardless of what you have been through, going through, or will go through to contend for your faith.

Why Do Some People Walk Away from Jesus or Foundational truths?

I've had the opportunity to minister or speak to individuals who have walked away from the Christian faith or do not believe in God. Instances include individuals who felt God did not answer their prayers. Some individuals were angry at God because of trauma or the death of a loved one. Others shared bad experiences with a ministry or ministry leader. Lastly, there were others that never experienced the power of God. Some just wanted to live according to their own "rules" or fleshly desires. In my opinion, I will summarize the excuses into four reasons: unbelief, unforgiveness, rebellion or deception.

Take a moment to evaluate if you are struggling in the issues listed above. If you are, confess these issues to God so He can forgive you and provide grace in your time of need according to His Word in Hebrews 4:16. This is a vital part of working out your salvation. Confessing your sins, receiving God's forgiveness and correction will prevent you from abandoning foundational truth and remaining in His love.

Contend Through Persecution, Trials & Tribulations

The Bible has a lot to say about persecution, trials, and tribulation. For example,1 Peter 4:12-19 says don't think fiery trials are strange. In 1 John 3:13, it states, don't be surprised if the world hates you. If you have accepted Jesus as Lord and Savior, you will suffer for righteousness's sake. But the Word tells us in 2 Timothy 2:12, *"if we suffer with Christ, we will reign with Him"*. Reigning with Christ means experiencing victory in your life now. It means fulfilling the will of the Father and trampling over the enemy. It means demonstrating the Kingdom of God on earth now. Therefore, I encourage you to contend for your faith and reign with Christ. In order to do that, tap into the power of forgiveness and praying for your enemies to be like Jesus!

The Power of Forgiveness & Praying for Your Enemies

It's easy to pray for those who love us. However, the challenge and real power comes from forgiving and praying for our enemies or for those who have mistreated us. When we forgive, God forgives us, and we keep a direct line open for His grace and strength to make it through our trials. Praying for our enemies keeps our hearts pliable. We please God when we pray and forgive our enemies. As we love our enemies, we demonstrate our faith and what we believe. We are able to receive help in a time of need and our prayers are not hindered. We can be confident that God has heard us, and we are not denied.

As we forgive and pray for our enemies, we are demonstrating the character of Christ in the midst of darkness. Philippians 2:25, AMP reads, *"So that you may prove yourselves to be blameless and guileless, innocent, and uncontaminated, children of God without blemish in the midst of a [morally] crooked and [spiritually] perverted generation, among whom you are seen as bright lights [beacons shining out clearly] in the world [of darkness]."* This is the perfect will of God, our Father!

Faith Without Works is Dead

As believers, we have the responsibility to demonstrate what we believe by our actions. After we are saved, God wants to live through us and complete works through us by His grace. We must surrender to God's will and allow Him to us. We must pray and intercede for our friends, family, peers, neighborhoods, etc. We must share our testimony with others so they would know the redemptive, transformative power of God. Visiting orphans and widows in their afflictions is another work. Once we are saved, we are to demonstrate what we believe by our faith.

Faith and work apply to every aspect of our lives. If you want to be an attorney, you must put in the work by going to school, studying, completing apprenticeships, and passing the bar exam. If you want to be a CEO of your own business, you must pair your faith and your work. This means creating a vision for your business, applying for your LLC (Limited Liability Corporation) and promoting a marketing plan. Put your belief in God's Word to work by sharing the Gospel of Jesus Christ!

Contend for Your Faith by Speaking Up

God has a platform or a group of individuals for you to reach. You will know when God has given you a platform to share Christ or minister to those in need. You will have opportunities to share your testimony. You will be moved with compassion to minister God's love, provide benevolence, or provide a word of encouragement. It could be anywhere, in your neighborhood or in the marketplace. It could be in prisons, shelters, or other organizations. You will be surprised how God can and will use you if you are willing to speak up. It may not be a long conversation, but a simple interjection of God's will or heart within your window of opportunity with an individual. Lastly, be on the lookout for divine appointments. Divine appointments are when the Holy Spirit leads you in the path of an individual to witness Jesus, intercede, bless, or share wisdom.

The Spirit of Disbelief

An unbelieving spirit is one of the most destructive strongholds you can have. The Free Dictionary defines **disbelief** *as the inability or refusal to believe or to accept something as true*. I believe contributing factors, such as trauma or hereditary disbelief causes a snare that allows the infiltration of the enemy to build a "fortress" or a stronghold of unbelief in the mind or heart.

Many individuals who have experienced trauma find it hard to believe in God, especially if their trust has been broken by people who claimed to serve or know God. Hereditary disbelief is simply what's implied; no knowledge or belief in God's Word within a generation. This could have happened because the family's bloodline was never taught or introduced to God's truth regarding God's purpose for man and salvation through Jesus Christ. Take a moment to evaluate if there are any areas of disbelief in your life. If so, find a scripture to counter attack your disbelief. This is a part of contending for your faith!

Rebellion - A Gateway to Destruction

Rebellion has caused many to leave God. Let me remind you, Lucifer was God's angel that decided to build his team and rebel against God. We know how that turned out. He was kicked out of Heaven and condemned to darkness. Rebellion has caused many to disregard God's Word and to live according to fleshly desires. When a person refuses to live by God's Word, the individual is saying in his heart, I know what your Word says but I choose to do as I wish. People living according to their will are more common now than ever.

The book of Jude identified these individuals as *"ungodly men, who turn the grace of our God into lewdness and our Lord Jesus Christ."* **Lewdness** is defined as, *wicked purpose, devices, or heinous crime*. The individuals Jude wrote about attempted to deceive and discourage believers from remaining faithful to Jesus Christ and living contrary to the Word of God. These instances are occurring today through individuals luring believers to practice acts of the flesh.

The Word of God warns us in Galatians 5:19-21 ERV. *"19 The wrong things the sinful self does are clear: committing sexual sin, being morally bad, doing all kinds of shameful things, 20 worshiping false gods, taking part in witchcraft, hating people, causing trouble, being jealous, angry, or selfish, causing people to argue and divide into separate groups, 21 being filled with envy, getting drunk, having wild parties, and doing other things like this. I warn you now as I warned you before: The people who do these things will not have a part in God's Kingdom."* To work out our own salvation, we must submit to God's authority, which is His Word. Living according to God's Word will save us from the dangers of rebellious behavior.

Dangers of Not Obeying the Word of God

There are dangers of not obeying the Word of God, such as reaping what you sow. To **sow**, means *to plant a seed or a substance that yields, grows, or produces its by-product*. To reap means to receive as a return, recompense, or results. The Bible says in Galatians 6:8 Amplified Bible (AMP): *"8 For the one who sows to his flesh [his sinful capacity, his worldliness, his disgraceful impulses] will reap from the flesh ruin and destruction, but the one who sows to the Spirit will from the Spirit reap eternal life."*

If we practice a sinful lifestyle, we will have a hardened heart. We are at risk of being drawn further away from the Heavenly father to a life of mayhem. **Mayhem** is simply, *damaging disorder or chaos*. A sinful lifestyle can cause an individual to become desensitized to biblical truths and begin to live in a backslidden condition. If anyone continues to live in a backslidden condition, eventually that individual can become reprobate. The Bible dictionary defines **reprobate** as, *"that which is rejected on account of its own worthlessness (Jeremiah 6:30; Hebrews 6:8; Greek: adokimos, "rejected")*. This word is also used with reference to persons cast away or rejected because they have failed to make use of opportunities offered them (1 Corinthians 9:27; 2 Corinthians 13:5-7)."

Another definition of **reprobate** from dictionary.com is, *"a depraved, unprincipled, or wicked person."* Living a life dedicated to righteous living is a key ingredient to contending for your faith in these times. Complete the following exercise regarding "Working out Your Own Salvation" on the next page.

Follow-Up Exercise

In your own words, describe what it means to work out your own salvation with reverential fear?

_____
_____
_____
_____

What are potential hindrances to working out your own salvation?

_____
_____
_____
_____

How will you put your faith to work?

_____
_____

Write down your final thoughts or key take-aways regarding Chapter 5:

CHAPTER 6

CONTENDING FOR YOUR FAITH AFTER TRAGEDY

Tragedies, trauma, and disappointments will happen in our lives or in the lives of our friends and families. You can say it's a guarantee. How you respond to tragedy will determine your destiny. I would like to share a tragedy our family suffered. It was the passing away of our daughter, Faith. My daughter was born prematurely due to myself needing an emergency c-section due to Eclampsia. They had to deliver our daughter early to save my life. Faith was born weighing one pound and one ounce. She lived in the Neo-Intensive care unit for three and a half months. This was the most trying time of our lives. We were in constant prayer. I fasted, prayed, and made decrees that Faith would live. I had prayer warriors praying. I was reciting scriptures. You name it. We did it.

During this time, our daughter had multiple surgeries. There were days of ups and downs. Our life was like a roller coaster. After her last surgery, the doctor's told us she was not going to make it. I did not believe their report. I still had faith in God. The next morning, she passed away. It was the most devastating time within our lives. After her death, our family was devastated. We had to accept the fact that our baby was not coming home and plan for her funeral service.

This was the most heartbreaking experience I've ever suffered. Before our daughter's service, I wrote a poem as part of the obituary, at the end. It read, Romans 8:28-39 (NIV) *"28 And we know that in all things God works for the good of those who love Him, who[a] have been called according to His purpose. 29 For those God foreknew He also predestined to be conformed to the image of His Son, that He might be the firstborn among many brothers and sisters. 30 And those He predestined, He also called; those He called, He also justified; those He justified, He also glorified."* During my pain, all I could do is remember that God is good, and He does change His mind towards me.

More Than Conquerors

A part of contending for our faith included remembering God's Word is true and that we were more than conquerors according to Romans 8:37. We had to remember that all things work together for the good, as it is written in Romans 8:28. Lastly, we must know that nothing will separate us from the love of God, not even the death of our baby according to Romans 8:38-39. It was easier said than done. Today, our family is stronger as we often remember that our daughter, Faith, is in good hands with the Heavenly Father.

Contending During Difficult Times or Tragedies

I want to be transparent. There will be situations or life events that will try to discourage or even crush you. There are so many people today that are not transparent and identify or discuss realities that happen during loss of a loved one. Everyone deals, processes or cope with the loss of a loved one or tragedies in different ways. My testimony is for the person who is still struggling with having faith in God, being at peace with what has happened in the past or stuck in a place of bitterness or grief.

An elder once told me, God loves Faith more than you do. He didn't want her to suffer anymore. God wanted her to come home. What she said made sense, even though I was still hurt. It brought me comfort. My sister Rita told me, just because Faith died, did not mean I had to let my faith die.

After the loss of my daughter, I went through the five stages of grief. I battled depression and suicidal thoughts. I felt like my breath was snatched away from my body. At that time, I felt that I would never pray a prayer of healing or deliverance ever again.

Having Faith to Pray for Others in Spite of my Own Loss

Years later, after my family received healing and restoration at our ministry, I was prompted to visit sick church members and pray for their healing and deliverance. I have even prayed for strangers regarding healing and deliverance during divine appointments everywhere. There have been countless testimonies of individuals who were healed from life-threatening ailments. The testimonies are too many to share. (These testimonies are for another book.)

After the loss of my daughter, God called me to become a spiritual "midwife" for several women in the Body of Christ. I was required to "labor" in prayer for babies to be secured in the womb and birthed. There were babies that were at risk of being miscarried or being born prematurely. I was able to pray and decree long life, health, and strength to these babies. As of today, I am pleased to report, these children are a blessing to their families. Some of these children are now adults, living out their purpose. The anointing of God is resting upon these children. Having faith to pray for others in spite of my own loss, stretched my capacity to a whole new level of intercession.

Of course, I had to overcome negative thoughts from the pit of hell, such as, unanswered prayers, unworthiness, fear, and unbelief. In the moments of interceding for others, I did not deny my faith in Jesus Christ. I still believed in the healing power of Jesus Christ, after the passing of our daughter. Since then, miracles were evident through Jesus to set people free, through healing and deliverance. Just imagine if I had walked away from Jesus Christ and no longer believed in the gospel of truth. Just imagine if I did not have faith to believe in a miracle, or healing for someone else because of my own tragedy. God would not have been able to manifest His power and glory through me. All glory be to God. He trusted me to demonstrate the Kingdom of God after I continued to walk in faith.

Complete the following exercise regarding, "Contending for Your Faith after Tragedy" on the next page.

Follow-Up Exercise

Are there any tragedies or traumas that occurred in your life that cause you to struggle in the area of your faith?

_____

_____

_____

_____

Why do you think it is important for you to contend for your faith after a tragedy or trauma has occurred in your life?

_____

_____

_____

_____

Write down your final thoughts regarding Chapter 6:

_____

_____

_____

CHAPTER 7

WE ARE CONTENDERS OF OUR FAITH

It's important that regardless of what happens in our lives, we make a conscious decision to live according to the Word of God and contend for our faith. I encourage every believer to live a consecrated lifestyle by being careful of what you feed your soul. Do not allow your eyes to view things which are evil, things which will cause you to sin. Do not listen to foolish teachings. Study the Word of God so your thoughts can be transformed to God's will. If you make a mistake, repent, and move forward. Plan not to live a life of habitual sin.

If you need to get granular with planning <u>not</u> to sin, do it. Set some time in your calendar to study and to pray. Get granular with who you will spend your time with. Set your radio station to only hear uplifting, "Word"-based music. Get rid of rated-R cable channels. Block websites that can lure you into lust and perversion. For some, it may be removing yourself from social networking sites. You know your struggles and where your temptation lies. Adjust your habits and plan to live victorious! On the next page, you are encouraged to write a decree of how you will "Contend for Your Faith" and walk in victory!

The Blueprint to Contend for our Faith to Impact the Next Generation

The Apostle Paul wrote a letter of exhortation to the Colossians to encourage believers to remain in Christ and grow in truth to avoid being deceived. Apostle Paul wanted all believers of Jesus Christ to know he was contending for them. The Apostle Paul contended for the Body of Christ through prayers, supplications, and spiritual warfare. The

Apostle Paul's New Testament letters to the early church promoted salvation in Christ. He dispelled false doctrine and challenged human traditions not patterned after Christ. Most importantly he provided us a blueprint for the Body of Christ to contend for our faith to reach future generations.

Our assignment in the Body of Christ is to remain constant in prayer and supplication for all believers that they remain in Jesus Christ and to "contend" through prayer, spiritual warfare, worship, preaching, teaching, discipleship, demonstration of God's power. We should continue to pray for the salvation of our loved ones, friends, and enemies according to God's Word in John 3:16-17, *"16 For God so loved the world that He gave His one and only Son, that whoever believes in Him shall not perish but have eternal life. 17 For God did not send His Son into the world to condemn the world, but to save the world through Him."* My prayer is that you are excited and encouraged to contend for your faith in these times!

In Jesus name, write your declaration statement of how you will contend for your faith on the next page.

Follow-Up Exercise

Colossians 2:6-7 God's Word Translation
"6 You received Christ Jesus the Lord, so continue to live as Christ's people. 7 Sink your roots in Him and build on Him. Be strengthened by the faith that you were taught, and overflow with thanksgiving."

Write your declaration statement of how you will contend for your faith below:

_____

_____

_____

_____

_____

Hebrews 10:20 says, *"Let us hold fast the confession of our hope without wavering, for He who promised is faithful."*

How will you contend for the faith on behalf of your family, friends, neighbors?

_____

_____

_____

_____

References

Articles:

Pope Francis Says All Major Religions Are Paths to Same God
https://www.prophecynewswatch.com/article.cfm?recent_news_id=50

More Americans Are Turning Their Backs on Religion, and Here's Why.
https://www.usnews.com/news/articles/2016-08-24/more-americans-are-ditching-religion-pew-study-says
Rachel Dicker, Associate Editor, Social Media | Aug. 24, 2016, at 2:03 p.m. Pew Research Center is a nonpartisan fact tank that informs the public about the issues, attitudes and trends shaping the world. We conduct public opinion polling, demographic research, content analysis and other data-driven social science research.

Definitions from Merriam Webster:

https://www.vocabulary.com/dictionary/gird
http://www.bible-dictionary.org/Reprobate

www.ingramcontent.com/pod-product-compliance
Lightning Source LLC
Chambersburg PA
CBHW072114290426
44110CB00014B/1904